ASYLUM SEEKER

ASYLUM SEEKER

Poems by Rich Murphy

THE POETRY PRESS

Los Angeles   Hollywood

THE POETRY PRESS

OF PRESS AMERICANA

americanpopularculture.com

Cover Photograph: Angela Stafford

Library of Congress Cataloging-in-Publication Data

Names: Murphy, Rich, 1950- author.
Title: Asylum seeker / poems by Rich Murphy.
Description: Los Angeles, Hollywood : The Poetry Press, [2018]
Identifiers: LCCN 2018002731 | ISBN 9780996777964
Classification: LCC PS3613.U7534 A6 2018 | DDC 811/.6--dc23
LC record available at https://lccn.loc.gov/2018002731

TABLE OF CONTENTS

In memory of Derek Walcott: "It takes aim."

Oh think twice, cause it's another day for
You and me in paradise
Oh think twice, it's just another day for you
You and me in paradise
               —Phil Collins

The phenomenon of "brainwashing" is eminently present nowadays in both propaganda and commercial advertising – though hiding under the politically correct names of "advertising," "broadcasting," "public relations," downright to "information service," and resorting to Joseph Nye's "soft," instead of "hard," variety of power.
               —Zygmunt Bauman

[L]ooking around us today, we see just what we might expect: we, "the world" would rather live through the misery of the reality we have created…than put together a new, negotiated reality.
               —Paul Auster

Courage of hopelessness means not renounce hope but get rid of the false solutions. Recognize a false solution that appears as a solution, but really it is a train moving toward you. That is the only way to invent something new.
               —Slavoj Zizek

If you assume that there is no hope, then you guarantee that there will be no hope. If you assume that there is an instinct for freedom, that there are opportunities to change things, then there is a possibility that you can contribute to making a better world.
               —Noam Chomsky

CHESTNUT FRAME

"It's the tree of life," Yossarian answered, waggling his toes, "and of knowledge of good and evil, too."

Milo squinted closely at the bark and branches. "No it isn't," he replied. "It's a chestnut tree. I ought to know. I sell chestnuts."

"Have it your way."

—Joseph Heller

Political scientists hung up lab coats and quit the experiment in the 1930s when the Founding Fathers Foundation fell into a great depression. Pitchforks made hay around federal government buildings and resurrected a body that stood between the money makers and the money spenders. Business men then went to work to define states, without unions, as united or at least possessed by a quiet desperation that the Soviet Union couldn't hide. The executive definitions may be why "[t]hree like terrifying political murders have cast, as Adam sighed, no shadow on the Whites' House."

When communism disappeared into the sunset in 1990, democracy followed, not in suit but in overalls, and the oligarchs who owned the work ethic exiled the precariat workers underfoot. Without representation, the refugees were permitted to become caddies because the harbingers of bad news could hold the billionaire's change, so as to envy and recognize that the poor are always embarrassed tycoons.

PSYCHOANALYSIS

Dog whistle, ear worm, media spoon-feed,
the utensils for the mask distributors
(Authenticity Inc.) that crossing-guards retire
when thought deserts into an adulthood elsewhere.

The canned conversation over vanilla
goes down and up easily for the consumer.
The tour guide walks with a child
and remains helpful to the big boy too.

While the dreams lead for the waiter and mother,
the Hedonist Reproduction Authority fiddles
with the crank organ and brass bells.

Teasing out cliché and non sequitur,
the thumb sucking inequity grows
into Goliath sitting on an unslung hero.

Plumbing the depths to count layers beneath
through orifices in the face in the mirror,
the archeologist surfaces long after,
speechless at the signs Bone Deposits & Co.
and the silent slack after that.

FRONTAL LOBE TO PSYCHOLOGY

With objects flattened into dollar bills
even nature rests in peace in green,
possessing for watermarks.
(The hunter and the deer aim to escape,
but both give way to legal tender.)

Eclectic in currency the city
shock treatment brings on patients
for adjustment into senselessness.
Stocked and bonded, accordions in work clothes
inhale after each crushing therapy,
learning to breathe to syncopated rhythms.
The music stresses and deforms.

The sheep loose to do as the admen wish,
the entangled inmate struggles
for freedom among jingo jingles
with every bleat from an automobile.

BRAINWASH

Scrubbed with DNA,
rinsed in mother fluids, the slate,
awaiting canal crown and chalk dust,
absorbs for bone and hard wiring.

Out of the socket where nurture settles
for lecture and training where coercion
and discipline toddle along,
rewards and punishment compete.

Where to find normal
on an accident-prone planet
spiraling toward genetic servitude
while poets search in pockets
for free will to stop an everlasting era?

BLUEPRINT FOR 2040

Salivating over double helixes,
engineers gape at sidewalk crowds
while glimpsing at master dreams.

Playing the ol' slide ruler
and fiddling with bow compass
and caliper, the Ob/Gyn Bands
mark time during fetal formation.

No stick needed; MacArthur
and Nobel carrots tickle
and scientific noses respond.

From inside out, from before
the chicken where eggs lay around,
bells and whistles introduce
to rave newt world: mini-paradise
for the parasite while serving.

PRIVATE PLACES

Secrets own no homes.
Closets contain orchestra pits,
balcony seating, concession stands.
Personality hangs by a lip;
a shadow by nails in the hall.
Should a bulge suggest a pocket,
DNA psychologists frisk for life.

Above the streets the NSA voyeur
moons, exposing pornography
to the touch screen cell phones below
that fulfill desire by the dominatrix.

Crowded with bathroom routines,
bedroom behavior, and sex acts,
the x-rayed marketplace reveals
big data spitting out crunched bones.

Town hall forfeits a space
for dialogue and persuasion
to spilled gut stories where honesty
performs on cue and compassion
spread eagles, arrested.

SECOND NATURE

The blink response confesses
as good deeds blanket

Second acts counter
but camouflage defoliates when understood

A Freudian slap in a courtroom

Denial pulled to a chin
warms until threadbare

The mind-reading sessions conspire
to tear, leak, deluge

Damning the shrink seams: useless

Caught on a meat hook,
dream often remains so;
responsibility looks for the tender loin

Fish stories end with flip-flopping

Guts suggest for two minds:
a saint walks across each stage

THE LEAP INTO LANGUAGE

On a tongue tip, the larynx leapt
from biology into language.
So Geronimo, whether cannon ball
or swan, impressed for listeners
who owned the code book.
The bestial kingdom danced
on all fours for generations
while the birds scaled
without sheet music.
At first, the brute forced with words.
Not far behind, sharp sticks
and bullets would hail
upon rock and fertile ground
giving rise to armies and banks
to sluice and funnel currency.
To dominate the indifferent cosmos,
the vacillator between fear and desire
begins at arm length.
Poems sometimes apologize insincerely
for hanging on to a lash or lobe.
With luck a parrot will squat
upon shoulders or a carrot
bounce before noses:
the war metaphor leads to the literal.
Without cooperation from stones
the totalitarian-in-disguise overthrows,
angry that the universe ignores for spite.
To remedy alienation,
a concentration camp for Coke and Pepsi
seeks out internal proletariats
and threatens with cleavers and ideology.

INSIDE OUT

Namely, that we're accidental pieces of flesh, mutton without
meaning.

—Zia Haider Rahman

An image of thought called philosophy has been formed
historically and it effectively stops people from thinking.

—Gilles Deleuze

Mutton without meaning,
Bo-Peep wakes in thought
while concepts with lids roll
and blink at the hard and fast:
rock, tree, hot top, the concrete.
Bah blah perhaps once packed
into an image a different world,
but rhyme or reason may
order or stew. Gödel and Einstein
deal in pupils at the bookstore.
A celebrity pushes at tear ducts
from across the kitchen table.
Fear and desire inspire, explore.
Furniture moves around rooms
depending on what school
or playground the shepherd attended,
what lesson comprehended.
Feng shui, ole! Feng shui, ole!
Sometimes, an idea inflates
in a cranium and a neighborhood,
a lifetime clings to the rubber inner tube
and not to empire and ego.

MILIEU FREIGHT

Along the zeitgeist train,
where contingency loops
to snag a morning, decade,
century, the change in the mood
in a nation eludes for scientists.

Test tubes and social engineers
come up empty when an eyedropper
from the blue drips into the day
as though managing the future
seams to the impossible.

However, the passengers remain.
Even the free thinker links
to the atmosphere when talking
in an effort to hitch arms together.

Paradigm plates may slip
within a genius who writes a look,
but how does the table overturn;
how do the mountains move
within a climate at city-center?

Mind-altering chugs tug and lug
around notions and countenances
to fashion and train direction
for the long nap on maps.
All aboard Spirit Express.

THE CLASSIC FILM ON COMMON SENSES

A mimicked gimmick coats with breath mint.
Wishes wrap in momentary certainties each morning
until clown shoes appear on sincere feet.
Panning for gold on city sidewalks,

pop-up entrepreneurs, precarious workers,
and midget marketing efforts extend for nickel;
Tambourines or tin cups mine best on streets.

Purse and pocket music squeak by for years
without ramshackle upending cries in fear.

History gauges hold that gadget and gismo construction
ate at despair, only to swallow up the rest.
Local whether dictates when hand and eye cooperate
or when thought and body coordinate.

"All experience hath shown that mankind are more disposed to
suffer, while evils are sufferable than to right themselves by
abolishing the forms to which they are accustomed."

And so the service selector service engages and marries
while gloom blooms and woes sadden into people.
The waiting station for the next us sits on a shelf, a sardine can.

Only when we arrive will fidgeting and twitching stop
and the opening for despondency hope in 3-D action.

BUSTLE HUSTLE

The gig jig weighs against the debtor
and journeyman alike, but wiggles
with a feather for the stock-holding
chief exploitation officer and beans spill.

Disposable people with wall-flower addresses
disappear into a dreaded truth:
taught to fear becoming.

The dance instructor in some corner office
choreographs three-step line jobs
for the denial states and whole psyches
slip on the electric slide: we.

Don't drink the Kool Aid and get high
and tangled within corporate structure?
Musicians tango with a one-horse carriage;
artists Van Gogh without either ear;
stock boys fetch when a distant whim wishes.

The fishbowl, filled with colored water and sugar,
waits on a giggle from the ice cube
who rigs all the angles from the board.

Unhappy with the exclusive arrangements
that promise cameo appearances now-and-again,
maybe next week, the crammers and jammers
post whole lives for sale.

RETAIL UMPIRE

In the purchasing cage,
the pitch machine for envy
catapults against the fall into desperation.
The barbarians with ownership
in mind and shaking trees in groins hurl.
The swinger and the mixed-up
batter on deck dance and duck
as product after product curve
and speed across a mock home plate.
Sometimes a dozen wallets can't dress
for and then attend to a ball.
Step sisters fudge with the equipment.
Other times the pelting with subliminal
effects hail down without a Louisville
slugger or mitt for catching fire.
Ignored by the team, excess coveting
under a cap explodes into debt
or with arms and fellow All-Stars.
Soon three strike-zone heaves
will foul to the locker room
where towel-snapping warps
into the hell, the irrelevant player.
Not positioned as opportunity
but as a cleat hanger, the costumer
in the right field fears the boos
and booze when freedom autographs.

HISTORY LESSENS

Defending champagne   bubbles,
Armed drones police

                         above the lanes

                              where barracks could burst

at any moment into mobs.

To maintain   the status quo offensive
     computer networks   fish to ensnare

the infra-red pinpoint   for insurrection
                         roundups by corporate security.

"Welcome into the world:
                    Trust fund babies to the right please;
Everyone else
          report to the tattoo station."

THIS SAD TIME WE MUST OBEY

Spells are all broken.
                    —William Shakespeare

The society everywhere is a living myth of significance of
human life, a defiant creation of meaning.
                              —Ernest Becker

1

The Black female protagonist and narrator
wakes alone in a fallow field.
A Caucasian woman sitting in a ditch
along the roadside continues
to gather facial expression toward composure.

Dusty, Mr. White strides up ahead
while a hobbling minor character,
a servant, attempts to catch up.

2

Over a riverbank, nine judges broke
the backbone in the great American novel:
bound chapters, torn, fluttered
about the days in the prison;
the Berlin Wall embedded
along the Mexican border;
and pages drifted upon an Indian
reservation, predicted accumulation, tribe deep.
A bald bird sails above crying out: "Fiat, fiat."

3

Once upon yet another exception
murderers and thieves in churches arrived
on the wind with promises to inhabitants.
Instead, enterprise = freedom = intruder weed
and crab grass from sea to sea.

4

"Read?" "No need!" The business plan.

Pop eyeballs slide into hypno-reenactment
via sandwich boards and consumer roles
for canned laughter and a chief demoralization officer.

If the mob can't gun down time
in broad daylight and before bed,
then why own it?

5

Besides, the mic used by Cronkite got lost,
and the slope into airwaves with anything as news
was forecasted and ignored under foot.

The game show Desublimation for the Precariat 24/7
possessed during work and at home too.
Alternate facts, unreason, and incivility
sit at the controls in studios.
"Truth" lies in Limbo
having survived the electric chair.

6

A charade took over the 9/11 and Wall Street
Fear Department before an appetite
could whet for revenge against the puppeteers.
The stew sickened
while the rise for the rest looked
to Main Street as though a sinkhole triggered.

Lost among the user-illusions,
the computer despair men
and every other hominid
occupying a continent in protest
reach for banisters and tools without handles.

7

Performing holy hand stands,
the totalitarian democracy sect
preys on and on: the money honey.

So unless a graffiti artist starts swinging
back and forth on a school bell
with all the elementary supplies
for contingency, the death knell
resides in tweets, twerks, and just do it.

SECTION NOTES

1. Outline of American fiction with Flannery O'Connor in mind

2. Citizens United court decision; Standing Rock; Elimination of the gold standard

3. Exceptionalism (American, British, Roman, etc.)

4. Aldous Huxley's *Brave New World*: "Why have time if you can't kill it?"

5. Herbert Marcuse's "repressive desublimation";" Zygmunt Bauman's "precariat."

6. Fareed Zakaria's book *The Rise of the Rest*; Daniel Dennett's "user-illusion;" Hannah Arendt's call to "think without banisters."

7. Sheldon Wolin's "inverted totalitarianism;" Northrop Frye's "three bells of literature."

BY THE LATEST TREND

The CEO, wearing plastic
leotards with a security coded cape,
seduces with leg and a snappy,
limp whip swiped from a customer
who was once always right.

(Every six months, saddled by shareholders,
the super hero puts up with stick-pin paper tails.)

After learning to serve envy,
the consumer grazes on the greenery
left by debt opportunities on television:
cookie jars bring no change to life.

The gulf between emulation and depravation
chews on confident moments, spits out
a leather sack stuffed with wasted time.

The leaves on trees don't convert to cash,
so a minimum wage invites
with precariat charm and sadistic hours.
Into the evening, employed knees
and resentful elbows creep
toward a curbstone pillow that winks.

Throughout the kingdom for slavery
self-blame and worship pose
for the record that determines forever:
eighty years for creation stolen without notice.

YOURS = MINE

When marketeers data-mine,
the innumerable veins, arteries,
and corpuscles respond only to *kleśas*,
so the pitchmen drill to confuse, alarm.
Cages jolt and helmet lamps blink
to morph senses into cents.
Without a scent, the inexperienced
money bag sits in shopping carts,
where eye-level jingles cry.
The intersection that negotiates
the esophagus and bowels flutter
with a thousand canaries
that drop into the sump.
The central nervous system
recovers only when the target
has been emptied: a lambskin
purse turned inside out.
A buck in the cross hairs:
a religious experience.
Gallows timbers witness.
To close a mind to plugs, hype,
and deposit raiders provokes
according to the mountain movers,
Bill Board and Buzz Ward.
How many lotus positions
hang in effigy at the breakfast table?
Decapitators move in next door
to brand a back side or go viral.
Dopamine fixes rage through frontal lobes,
while episodic memory occupies in the cortex,
conducting for a sympathy across synapses.
Stripped to acid runoff and tailing mud,
the barren shopper arrives at the landfill.

THE LAM

Under the bus, the cry babies
distract for culprit getaways:
the slopes, the beaches,
the off-shore accounts.

Responsibility-sops makeup
the headlines for cops
the way mother did beds
and lullabies, while
absorbing eyes for publishers.

The commuters lost in news sites
on public transportation
don't respond to the bumps
in the road or the alarm clocks
that bring day or catastrophe.

Bread crumb trail stand-ins,
pop-up guilty plea figurines,
and excuse-laden alibi legal teams
cover for the never known.

PATRON TO THE RICH

Stock shelves, sweep floors,
and flip burgers: the philanthropist
sacrifices a living wage
to fund greed projects.

Then, guilty venture investors
and corporate board members
wishing to sprout wings,
build onto hospitals,
and attend to the 12-generation
recovery program for withdrawal.

The giver ghost hovers around the city
without until an election-time need
for manipulation heightens:
the capital and commodity creator
counts in the press and in statistics
among the living to add for victors.

The donor and Good Samaritan
eats and sleeps up to the chin in debt.
In a slum without escape or car
the aid worker and Santa Claus
patches together the day for children
or lives in shoes while seeking shelter.

THE "BRAND NEW" SYNDROME

Man is not the lord of beings. Man is the shepherd of Being.
                        —Martin Heidegger

Are you there for the pretender?
                        —Jackson Browne

1

Shepherding becoming among industrial
complexes and strip mall prison lots
upon each island Shifting-Baseline,
the culture orphan imagines and studies.

Alongside pathways, wolves chew on
possible careers and character traits.

While sons and daughters parade around
found objects and spirits
up and down volcanoes,
the marooned urchin with horn and staff
plots out what societal archipelago,
what erupted stepping-stone present,
may be next; gathers together evidence
that illuminates the journey so far.

2

The degeneration maps fit stuffed
where the generations gap.
Within the cosmos for struggle
(where the impossible plays on the beaches
surrounding the epoch),
class learners teach in order
to exit envy and greed for new emotions.

The in-order suspension
bridges over to each paradise,
slipping to and fro the nervous systems,
and pretends at problem-solving:
the feeding tubes for vocal cords
sway in the wind, wobble under foot.
Feel that.

3

The unborn dreams spend for cash
cold parents just as the sperm and egg,
once together and breathing,
dish out little change
in behavior stranded on
yet another uncharted Eden.

Washed up according to shipping reports,
the historian and tomorrow refugee
frightens to win a meadow for augury:
looking to get even
with the man selling a vacuum
the free loader stands on grounds
and kicks up dust.

4

No flight without death or conga line
from where science meets money-makers:
once boredom sets in and game means murder,
tall grasses and brush pant for a shore thing.

Barrel picking psycho-paths
around government R&D sites
define and redefine to suit nature

in convenient strait-jacket ties and lacings

for a synapse chasm where side-effects print
and neurons take notice.

5

The homo-sacer herdsman
rounds up sensibility and know-how
for staying behind on the tectonic fault
or crossing at the paradigm cliffs
(interregnum interregnum)
via Odysseus escaping from a cave.

6

Open fields need not steady or
lose to past and future as an isthmus
selects before the Red Sea rises and collapses.

Where the leaps step into a clearing,
a continent, the huckleberry imagination
that relies on the store-housed lessons
insists on educating the dictator, biology.

7

The sheep that alert senses to predator
and to discovery in the day and night
configure and bleat so that art appears.

Until eyes and ears callus into shale
or fall from the head one-by-one
and the craft sinks into a slow wave goodbye,
the emergence soil ushers and guides.

CARLSBAD HOTEL AND FLOP HOUSE

Compartmentalized in the elite brief case
one finds: union organizer repellent;
hypno-headphones with replacement
hot air pillows;
matching cliché-filled thought balloons;
undercover fringe benefit service brochure;
"no alternative" sound bites
for hunger pangs;
an axe handle;
and a shifting-baseline-syndrome applicator
substituting for a public school history book.

The shrunken tool box
for the precarious worker contains:
spikes for morning coffee
to empty the event-horizon;
hospitality uniform for the underemployed;
scurry sneakers and too big to fail
snack bags and soda bottles;
congratulatory scribble on note paper
two decades old;
well-moisturized tear ducts;
Hero brand Fix-It hypodermic needles;
and a percussion instrument for shortcuts
around dialysis machines
a cold pistol nipple
or a temple revolver.

Down the road the Habsburg spas stretch.

WEARING IDENTIFICATION

With work clothes stripped,
the mirror-image refuses
to identify the lump in clay.
Retiring the trade for someone made,
a pimple in the universe grovels
in gravel for meaning, bedrock.
In dark times that include daylight
adolescent cowards huddle
to satisfy with means merely.
Shops and calculators buck
until Earth shakes, quakes.
Bare back and fists filled
with mane come closest to daily groins.
The grind greets with humps,
clumps, and bumps in red earth,
yellow earth, black earth,
and white earth for meeting.
Still, the roles in the period play ease on,
and in the hay loft the stick figure
disappears in a shirt. Look out!
The scare crow claims to own,
and nightmares fly into the sunset.
Then, puttering possesses
and a ghost pulls at sleeves
until a wrinkle swallowing stops.

FATAL FLAWS

Deformed by punctuality,
the boardroom-brags drag
against vacations, while
hands to a clock go 13 rounds
with punching bags.
The daily calendar shirt buttons
with appointments that tuck
press into disappointments,
and every hour gnarls
with last minute meetings,
coffee, and delegations.
At the club-footed golf game
where alarm apps
and disarmed abs substitute
for stick-pins, forked tongues
numb better than drugs.
A housewife disfigures
when making each pit stop
in a wheelchair school bus.
The entrepreneur and homeless
escape with a missing ear,
a ravaged nose, and one eye out:
a grain no longer an hour or flower.
Hunched over another dollar,
the zeitgeist panic rehabilitates
to acclimate to artificial rhythms
for organs, limbs, and turf.

PATRIOT ACT

In the 1960s, Seligman devised a theory of "learned helplessness." He found that a state of passivity could be induced in dogs by giving them repeated and inescapable shocks.

—Tamsin Shaw

With a 300-million cast
on set or at the panoramic scene
NSA directs with DARPA know-how
and a nose for amateur rivals.

Police sniff to snuff-out integrity.

From K-12 and in college too
entrepreneurs learn with expert intent,

so helplessness (only to be punished later)
steals for the show with a stutter.

In a terror state that calls the shots
at the Drone Theater and Observatory
bit actors perform (live for now)
for corporate audiences
that do the judging:

silence applauds; on location
a spotlight may "boo" to the stars.

SURVEILLANCE FOR ANY ERA

The gatekeeper between tomorrow
and yesterday contributes to the violence
in the current and lends to frame
for understanding events.

While the gut response to lightning
and elements wishes to remain innocent,
gauze weaponizes into tools.
The school master with a bull whip
upon the horizon experiments
with pedagogy to tame the whole landscape.

Anybody in the hospital without a scalpel
or mop declines on a gurney.
Background brutality polices
for the global accident under the sun
and with the deliberative devil in details.

Without attention to the props and scenes
symptoms hush for a moment
while the disease oppresses and the objective
bull eye targets and neutralizes.

At the border crossing, where a total
system follows a hodge-podge entourage
and passes over through now, the guard plants
while frisking and stepping aside.

At the factory for consent,
the friendly-fire in false flags
rolls in war-fog banks to confuse
human shields without credit.

The production-line workers
from state to stage sing and pounce
to keep voters off the streets
to keep feudal walls futile.

Unfurled on both sides,
collateral damage waves
at the conveyor belt that swaggers
this way and that for engineers.

Filled with emotion dressed in reason,
pitch men greet alongside store shelved
promises that whistle and explode
with fantasy for bargain hunters.

Stick-pinned cities on a map
numb for empire reaching,
until Operation What Next stuns
within dominion and truncates.

LACTATION NATION

When crying hungers in living rooms,
fear leaks from the nipple,
and mother cradles to secure voter lips,
the excuse for empire.

Spoon-fed broadcasts
meet up with a teething show
and run down from chins
onto bibs for cynics.

Mistaken for the couch occupant
by eyeballs and ears
that cushioned lingo confuses,
national security interest
slouches in electronic devices.

Crude, raw materials, and precious metals
under villages in Africa belong
in automobiles or cell phones
owned in peaceful neighborhoods overseas.

Standing in for the poor children
(old enough to know better)
the masters over money and minerals
dislodge from future refugees' tantalum
and then school to enslave.

FEED FORCES

The junk thought diet
sticks to tongues and cortex
and doesn't burn off
at the gym or at the dentist
magazine rack.
Jingles, jokes, and platitudes
canned for any occasion
fatten heads
while intellectual malnutrition
chews at bones.
Theorems with memorable
and impressive lexicons
trickle down,
but education that means
business uses fire hoses
to soak mountain peaks
with syrups for the lowest
common denominators.
If a mickey concoction
from a bio lab lad
or environmental text message
boosted IQs,
bowling alley eye balls
would mind Ps & Qs.
Parroted customer greetings
compete with emoticons
as brain food.
Peanuts in pockets
tame the elephants.
Everywhere the obtuse diagonals
confound: osmosis hocus-pocus
distracts focus.

IN THE MORASS

With a start beneath two brows,
the digestive tract sucks up
to the low hanging fruit
(Venus, Mars) while rumbling
through desire spitting pits
and dumping dreams behind.
The essential prune
for the paradise and host toast.
When lips part to coax
and the esophagus stretches
a neck, intestines prepare for
determination and advertises
a place to park natural resources
…forever: yoga mogul.
Worming a way through
everything outside the human body,
wit hands off the idea
to cold calculators.
Tick workers dismantle
and build to spec monstrosities
in a belly, Humvees strip-teased
into plows and addressed again
vice with verse. Never satiated,
the python continues to spy,
to conjure, to swallow and to parse
for use. Use: practical applications
and a narrow marrow in breath.

REALITY CHECK-POINT

Throughout a gaslighted nation,
the civilian audience focuses on
the wall inside military helmets.

A moral compass lost to vertigo,
shadows amass on borders,
threatening the living room chair.

Only a bullet hole through steel might reveal.
For the emotion engineers
hypno-media for hypnopedia construct
the American-mind into a police state.

False consciousness misidentifies
so that offshore may account and accrue
debtors while lids and limbs
twitch to prove existence.

The brainwashers scrub
with intimidation soap operas
and rinse in brain-bending poverty
before dirty laundry hangs:
better to delude than to include.

AN ALZHEIMER BANK ROLLED IN

Loitering outside taxpayer brain-labs
with hat in hands, the entrepreneur
picks up the gold coins thrown
to the ground by government workers.

When the businessman has manufactured
enough for interest in a certain glow
on the purchase button, pop culture
buys another self-made man.

The mannequins lie through passers-by
teeth that smile in envy.
The crowd in the stadium
had more to do with DARPA
than the concession stand fan thought.

The secret remains deep in the US
with so many contraptions rushing
around town and now in the air
that even the flag waver remains in a fog.

FROM THE VALE FOR A SOUL MAKING

O keep the dog far hence, that's friend to man.
>—T.S. Eliot

We like huddling in gangs and knowing / the exact time
>—W. H. Auden

"Eternity in an hour"
>—William Blake

10

Within the nose cone,
during the last moments for propaganda,
before the middle-ear implant,
before the genetic engineering,
and while the monkey tree remains rooted,
the poet speaks from a limb to human spaces.

9

Bracing against what blows in the wind,
the corporate scaffolding for the fuselage
siphons into the fuel containment vessel
from la durée, health, and retirement plans.

The limited resources in the fool chests
aim for the great unknown.

8

A ruler thrust into personal experiences
parries into a billion cruel chunks
to dictate into the universal trajectory:

"Wait for a minute, a second,"
muttered Interior Design, Inc.
"Open; say Aaaaaah." "Simon says zoe."
Say homo-sacer.

Surgically replacing sensory organs
with stones and tired treaded
lassitude for ligaments,
neglect numbs, and nimble nimble
intuitive responders
and passion lump into the world.

The user illusion swallows
and lifetimes disappear,
replaced by protein robots.

7

When the booster rockets
fall away and the skyscrapers
shake off the atmosphere
that may doubt, the empire state
helmets for the citizens.

Gestalt switch thrown,
the shifting-baseline-syndrome inoculates
through the denial system against past narrations.

6

The hit and run drive to add
to matrix communism marches on.
A watch worn with the face turned
toward the wrist, a mutating species
working with no lunch pail, flattens.

Operating the hunch pump,
fellow culture orphans plumb
to expose the brand new that plagues,
within the housing atop the spacecraft.

5

In the command module that language builds
belief installs for flooring and windows,
for walls and for thalamus.
The inkling and imagination siblings
had once grown up inside
as life-long-playdates-until-the-grave-date.

4

The raw flesh functioning for false-consciousness
cracks between sleep and awakening:

growing still in stature the grim Shape
Towered up between me and the stars,
and Strode after me;

It was the steeple of Saint-Hilaire
that gave all the occupations, all the hours,
all the viewpoints of the town their shape,
their crown, their consecration;

father said a clock slays as long as it is being
clicked off by little wheels;
only when the clock stops
does time come to life; and

when these new memories suddenly came upon me
…time had been placed in reverse.
As if, for that moment, the river ran upstream.

Now games for children: hunt the zipper.

Capsules for archeologist litter for ritual lozenges.

3

The internal personal inclinations
lose against the Big Ben,
the constant numbering on the touch-screen.

Upon the "our," the rhizome-under-the-oak-tree
gives up vital organs and vapors called thinking.
The hawk, the zombie,
and the self-possessed residing between
rise to the occasion: tuning fork precision.

When spotlighted, each audience member
opens to balcony-evil.
On stage, the villain sings with love
in a voice so that banal ears drink in the music:
the chorus meme, 23 + a "me-me."

2

The antics in the mind struggle
between monkey see monkey do
and leading for the tomorrow mimesis.
How much mob mimicking to remain
a member and where to break up habit
to win only the gift
from the empathy-mime, perhaps.

The relentless hacking at the stumped,
who possess limbs and imagination
(the parentheses threshold into privacy),
by face and hands counting down we.
From scratch pad to too big to fail generator,
the division for the Humanity,
the last stand on Earth:
rubber soles, optional.

10. Tree of knowledge and eternal life

9. Henri Bergson's "la durée"

8. Daniel Dennett's "soul making"; Giorgio Agamben's "homo sacer"

7. Ian McHarg's 1969 manifesto *Design with Nature*

6. Daniel Dennett's "intuition pump"; John Berger's "orphan."

5. Martin Heidegger's "language is the house of being"

4. William Wordsworth's *Prelude*; Marcel Proust's *In Search of Lost Time*; William Faulkner's *The Sound and the Fury*; Julian Barnes' *Sense of an Ending*; Aldous Huxley's *Brave New World*

3. Gilles Deleuze's and Jean-Jacque Rousseau's ideas combined. Hannah Arendt's idea of evil; "23" chromosomes

DEAD SEE SCROLL

Having raced to the brain-stem bottom,
sold eyeballs, cogs engage in a canyon
for technology that spits out lifetimes
onto couches and sidewalks.
A precipice and bungee cord place well after.

The starting blocks wedge between senses
and the world when a baby finishes a first cry.
The steeper inclinations frustrate with grade school,
and the machinery chews up higher education.

Where enlightenment breaks again and again
and the horizon divides darkness,
geared up for fun, addicts dive into phones
and drown in one gulch, pulled under
by coltan flywheels and user illusions.

Without assemblage ability, except for thumbs up,
the precarious meme mogul memorizes.
Sprouting ear buds and sporting a Bluetooth,
the obedient emoticon steams a glass plate.

GOOGLE DIRECTION

Replaced with emoticons,
the moral compass dizzies
among refrigerator magnets,
suffers from the needling.
The upturned lip-corners with teeth
required for consideration
apply to involved parties also
during secret assaults by superiors.
A good day storms even when
the wheelhouse pitches black.
To feign innocence,
the kitchen appliance owners
watch for the sun.
Contractors and wannabe politicians
hollow out the last infrastructure
and local aid can-dos with soup spoons,
while the street resident suffers
for tipping the bowl. Headlines
and sound bites substitute for thinking:
soldiers divine with hickory butts
to free precious materials
from beneath backward villages.
A smart phone tickles with banality
after exhausting indebted outrage
among job sites (bumper to bumper,
sidewalk crawls, and apps).

DIGITAL DIGS

Where the sunshine ends,
technology masquerades as democracy:
cybernetic shadows until blackout.
Social media pulls at the senses
to terrorize with tunnel vision
and friends in a mirror.

Eyeballs sop into palm tools
and bodies bury under information;
ghosts haunt from earbuds
just above sidewalks.

Practical jokes and news mingle
until the escapee succeeds
from seduced selfie to cartoon.
When city and country life stop
showing up for light breakfasts
and brilliant lunches, cave walls define.

The funnel into metaphor provides
for the body including a slave wardrobe.
Wander into the streets
to win envy and the yoked
and blackmailed chattel
entice for ignorance and not for a day.

THE POT-BOILER PARABLE

Short fiction, memoir chapters,
tall tales, tragic tones, mimes —
enemy to the ordinary —
The Narrative Gravity Center,
a break-even concern, juggles
for the charity Save-the-Child.

Antidotes for anecdotes,
the poisons pouring
from poor-choice misdeeds,
emotions pulling at bones,
or from the blue.
(space station)
Mars, Saturn, Jupiter with moons,
Venus lash to a heart, tongue tied by eyes
into a hope rope to a brilliant smile:
variations on a code, for a chord,
a cord to find the body, if not an ego.

On the sidewalks where each could also
drop a library on toes
a bibliography greets in boots
pathological liars in clown shoes.

If a line for sticking to tells all,
the poverty performs in greater pageant.

Sentenced by will,
after tripping over a rock,
the prisoner hammers
at an orbit obit on a story-straightener
when other cares around the globe
shrug off the denouement dust.

THE BANALITY DRAMA

During the catastrophe, the chorus
members rehearse until, but not for, death.
Lead victims may fix to a smile in the end
while collateral damage continues to cry.

By attending to acting lessons,
the cast imitates while masking
against children choosing uniforms in public.
The shrinking prison pants at the prospect.

When close enough to perfect,
the discipline dandy streets credibility.
Mere intimation opens for the fraud
who owns, worships, and rests on morale.

The jobber patches for need,
points toward idols and adapts to hobbies:
the authentic nobody tags dangle,
unprized from around the noosed necks.

Names seem to hold the singers decaying
among dogs and cats in the alley.
Ground between Earth and moon, the stars
at every stage fold over in character, tada:

at the catastrophe theater banality plays at now.

THE GIFT FROM THE GLASS-BLOWER

Peering into the globe with a giggle,
local populations admire and envy.
As though a crystal ball with backdoor
would open for one in thousand
and some Ali Babas, mom and pop
wait in living rooms to dance with the stars.

Teens plot outrage that comes with status
and with a prison sentence if necessary.
Neighborhood survivors settle
for poverty, television, and whatever
falls from the sky, while dreaming
for fame and washing in Technicolor.

Few and far between, light bulb revelations
rest with magic lantern hopes and frustration.
Shaking, rattling, and rolling the world
around the viewers left to devices,
temper tantrums and civil disobedience
give rise to and bring about confetti constellation,
consolation for later mimes and memes.

GLOBAL SOCIETIES

When the chicken dances
on the hotplate for fifteen minutes,
the frog comes to a boil in a pot,
and will set for serving.

From under the mind-business bubble,
where big money accumulates
(when given any chance), the sideshow
"under-glass" appears, at best,
among just deserts for poor choices.

The flame licking at the watched vat
grows with each austerity package
and unfunded local program.

The myopic minority celebrates
with fluted fizz beneath the ozone dome
and with kisses blows to the splash, cupola,
and effervescence tomorrow promises.

THE TUB SUDS SOAP OPERA

...living always means building spheres, both on a small and a
large scale, humans are the beings that establish globes and look
out to horizons.

—Peter Sloterdijk

In the bubble-bath each soapy globe
magnifies and small desires seem
(pleasure now and now and now   )
until the champagne campaign fizzles still
with an old promise: one flute filled with birds.

Tepid and discolored, b-minor freedom muddies
with mini-lives coated in film negative:
liberty lather blather.
A baby cries in the backyard.
A new car sits in the driveway.
The house owns for 30 years.
The dog froths at the messenger.

Bathers run round, circumspect about pins,
about porcupines, to hose down
soap-balloon lovers and patio grillers.
A chill towels with goose bumps:
flip flop pop.

According to the International Institute
for the Wind, the dents and dings
in trumpet bells blurt out,
"only accordions spring back to life."

THE LITERAL ELITE PARASOL

Predestined, the central intelligence agency
umbrellas for a nation
and then further for the world
so as to shelter noses stuck to atom clusters
against the metaphors that pelt and the bake.
The concrete crowd ducks under
whenever being reports danger ahead
and images seem to come from the blue above:
hands fill with railings and banisters.

At open Mike night,
Hurricane Gus howls a rib cage inside-out,
and everybody gets exposed to Art,
an old friend to tonsils
and the question mark that soaks or burns
and that lurks in everything.

By daylight engineers respond
to stretch a weatherproof canopy
to adjust the tool handles from the bedroom,
to the kitchen, garage, and public byways
and to replace the grips and triggers
with less tactile sensors in the "waker."

CONSTELLATION CONSOLATION

With an aurora on both shoulders
and a hello ringing Houston,
the angel astronaut whispers
for joy a blueprint upon Saturn.

The pearly fate vaporizes
at the tail fin in flight.

A gold rush salvation
with god beams via the clouds
lures real estate brokers and boon men,
so mined chunks from heaven
traverse across hostile atmospheres
to the measured utopia, a haven.

Satellites moon from devils the evils:
D for details.

Zipped Zoot suits with glass globes
and oxygen tanks haunt for life asteroid altars
and crater catacombs.

The jumps for ploy
and the giant step

for minerals straddle upon a desert planet
that deserts desperation.
Those angles, transcending
religious altitude, torque in retrospect
to ride over a present that make-shifts history.

DISTANT DESTINY

The foreground distracts
from the dark recesses
swallowing. The spotlight
strips tools from the actor.
No peep show exposes
the naked belly in the beast.
(A genuine smile hangs
in a wardrobe for play.)
The bully-mammoth
overwhelms any teeth
baring by hambone
or audience. A swinging
watch chain creates a fuss
so a monkey crawls into
the blank stare and takes over
behavior: drags knuckles,
drops a jaw, and drools.
Paint splashed onto props,
extras mobbing the set
rescue the protagonist
when a scene materializes.
A moment later not even
a gulp rolls under foot.
Only a hodgepodge
called memory clears
the esophagus for a tongue.

LIVING DEAD DISSENT

In the midst of beings as a whole an open place occurs. There is
a clearing in the woods.
>   —Martin Heidegger

After logic has pinned
non-science open for translation,
economics rampages
through the clearing in the woods.

Any alternative deep down things
explored through a dale with sun
suffer smear from desperate arrogance.

The trampled interior, mood and state,
by data idolatry and innovative pandering
gives birth to defective "am nots,"
while expanding death as a kingdom.

Counterfeit emotions
traumatize intrinsic anxiety and guilt
and paste in patterns
two-dimensional crowds
onto meadows and rocky peaks.

Wallpaper developers
in bed with corporate behemoths brag.

"If you don't get this,
you are a nobody," the mannequin says.

Every irrational moment
comes with a patch kit.

At culture control centers
futuristic rhapsodies inebriate
from myriad platforms and shift

54

the disgrace from nature to the past.
While frequency dominates,
force diminishes, and soft mantras
coat the psyche in salve and excuse
as the savvy avoid adulthood.

INCIDENTS FOR IMPROV

The waiting room at the dentist
holds more ache and pain per minute
than the self-inflicted and patient
in a week in the room for doubt —
and bus drivers pull teeth!

Always down the hall and to the left,
in the closet for second thought
the carpet and furniture never wore out.
Few were kept hanging.

Once a library, the time to hesitate
and take a breath sits on a lap
difficult to access, impossible to dwell in.

The architects don't draw on the past
but erase questioning, generate response,
post no fishing sighs against curiosity
where pondering could take place.

Kneejerk reactions keep the pace up
and the line moving to stampede Willy Nilly.

LYING AROUND

Pulling up and buttoning banality,
the shirk and skirt tuck in responsibility
below the belt exposing majority
rule for camouflage, long sleeved.
Bob and Weave enter the address
"Good Morning," and counter two
secret votes with aid and comfort for violence.
Ideology absorbs colors and patterns
so that shirts and dresses
make every occasion tyrannical.
The fabric for wardrobes survives
hanging and folding over at the gut,
looms quietly monitoring behavior
on continents, at sea, and now in outer space.
A painter, naked, could stretch
what passes for the truth
and shepherd bolder hues, but threads
change routines or not.
Every fiber about being seems to own empire.

LOUNGING MEDITATION

On a clear-conscience couch
in an underwear climate
memory stretches for the surf
through foamy old age to death.

Too late for the analyst,
the lefty in a yogi pose
lies without risking
for the historical now.

Bit-part fantasies occupy
while distraction tackles,
pins down the less experienced;
the body practices for the box.

No shame alarms toward
a dawn for contribution,
no body animated for teaching
in the street, as though

the future needs little
from the past and leaps up from here.

SAND TRAP

Oceanless, a golf ball terrorizes
with just enough space
for instant communication:
a worst enemy reaches out with a missile;
a kinder foe fumbles and the end!
Where a phone call may have driven
the point home, shock and awe explain.
The whole in won disputes,
groundless but real enough,
forgets that desire pains
on the backside with "more."
The masseuse without discipline
kneads while the handy cap club
calls to order the green keeper.
Experience might suggest
among borders and outer space
— a net, pool pockets, foul line —
that Zen pings into pong.
However, the teeming pursuit
to compete against continues with a streak
for manicured people on Astroturf.
The Hippy Dip weathered
into a speed bump among
artificial heart, artificial intelligence,
and artificial flowers. However,
dry-docked and then moth-balled,
fleets stand ready to turn clocks
back to steamer or frigate.

PROZAC POSITIONING VICES

The excess powerlessness infects
during the night when frustration
backs up and emotion overflows.

Each morning TINA and the gang
swarm through the city streets
with pitchforks, torches, and nooses
upending to find the dynamo director.

Plant and bestiality engineers turn
and hightail to deep depressions
three states away from commuting routes.
The jarred psyches in the root cellars
fertilize for fields at the university.

Bedridden with fever, philosophers
can't imagine outside Utopia.
Outed social scientists drinking castor oil,
pledge to technocracy and findings enrich.

Only a poet born in a Franciscan monastery
could leave behind bread crumb coordinates
to a tomorrow without moral bankruptcy
and Penia threatening at every turn in the road.
The wheel for fortune sweeps up
the compass pieces for politicians.

THE NOBILITY OF OUR EXISTENCE

The only way to deal with an unfree world is to become so absolutely free that your very existence is an act of rebellion.

—Albert Camus

1

The MLK Will and Testament

I think one of the big things that happened was that when black people began to be anointed by the trinkets of this capitalist society and began to become big time players and began to become heads of corporations; they became players in the game of our own demise.

—Harry Belafonte

Imported from Africa,
the farm animals sweated
under bullwhips and tree limbs
and bled-out bullets only
to earn trinkets awarded
by banks desperate for debtors.
Dancing at the end, where hope
once synched around a neck,
the framed face knows
more about struggle than
pale feet could imitate,
try as privilege does with might.
Up from slavery to consume
substitutes for the prize
when poor people pupils
with something to teach
in the streets wait
to meet human eyes.

2

Who the Hell is Diane Nash?
                    —RFK

What I've always been looking for: where resides the rebel heart?
                    —Harry Belafonte

Laying eye beams aside for now,
chewing nails first thing.
Room for a rebel takes stock:
hammered home experience,
saw what, blue print read, would.
A Franciscan poverty vow
fills for the work day.
Fields for soccer, rugby, football
may not do soon.
The heart beats from inside
the chest demanding out,
and by March and a discipline
in a spring a simple Simone will
pounds at rock and timber,
on the polis door.
Should cream color on walls,
Obi-Wan through Luke,
chapter and verse,
versus the Empire.

3

The Rebel Communion

We just have to get our old coats, dust them off, stop screwing
around and just chasing the good times, and get down to
business; there's some ass kicking that has to be done.
                                        —Harry Belafonte

Building a church on Standing Rock,
third from the sun, the Sioux sue
to continents: "Come over and help us,"
Sisyphus crying out for strange love,
for formulas for optimism,
for courage and intelligence
for rainbow warriors.

Over low-intensity oppression
and couch squatters hiding from activism,
through theoretical equality that conceals
great factual inequalities,
around murderers transformed into judges
to assure that no martyrdom occurs,
"to where the future is the only kind of property
that the masters willingly concede to the slaves,"

to indigenous, indigenous, indigenous

and global innocence responds with outrage.

RHIZOME CALL

Buried beneath the demand to waste
in attics, in basements, and on curbs
repressed need rots for no roots.

The lack inventors convey on belts
for owning and emaciated emotions
purchase to trash a slightest desire.

Delight in servitude answers
for the sacred word hushed
to prevent deed from entering limbs.

During the call for rhizome,
the gardener seeds against illusion
without growing disillusioned.

WATCHING HORSE RACES

We are the disc jockeys of an advanced technology.
                                        —Gayatri Spivak

Straddling the humanities,
disc jockeys settle at the starting gates.
The groove around the track
waits for the bell and for the bets
on a next generation from technocrats.
With whiplash consent for silky transition,
the little man perches on a saddle
to flap for children for whom
a same old song shines untouched.

A rocker somewhere dances
back and forth on a Yankee estate.
From the coliseum perhaps
a diseased brain and heart
fasten for the stirrups of course.
History, the broken record for some,
can't be beaten by woken
mortals competing, even with values
harnessed to pure science.

A line, phrase, word may flee,
as in moccasins, to invent
for freedom without illusion or irony.
During a reservation in Cheyenne country
another yet unbroken imagination
stands without a brand
wobbling around a breath.

MIME FIELDS

In the mine field for the insane
silence reverberates in hushes
here and there.
Personalities haunt where sticks
in mud celebrate victory.
The flash from possible worlds
disappears into quiet phantom limbs.
Flailing reflex prefixes,
homes drooling for occupants
slip by unpronounced
and so unvisited, tripping
titters at the tattered tacking
to cast-a-Blanca.
Articulation from the unknown region
falls among deaf ears,
occupied buildings in fields for study.
Know-it-alls follow in cities
that coordinate lessons learned
again and again.
The parade within right thinking
labels within pathology along a way.
Forks in roads spoon into soup.

DOMESTICATION

While one country mows the lawn,
a new state mops up along a border,
and crossing guards from united
nations enter into foreign streets.
The chores and honey-dos
that globalism tags to refrigerated
military trucks seek to check
and then neutralize in neighborhoods.
Bullies and deviants rake sidewalks
or leave for the hillsides. Hegemony
swallows and with water a bitter pill
dissolves into ideology. A television
performs in living room where
physical therapy satisfies. Big data
looks down upon noses
while unbuttoning blouses.
The veteran consumer sleeps
in a house built from statistics
as the homeless continue
fighting over corrugated cardboard.

PROVERBIAL NEW

Where clichés comfort,
headstones should alarm,
though the earth tucks
and hugs all around.

Outside the cemetery,
the mine fields for the insane
blossom with possibility
for original language.

Just beyond rut-ridden nouns,
if one distrusts the pop-psychologists,
the distant quiet and thunder
articulate with a strange rhythm.

When a waked and now woken
jingle hummer nurses around an ear,
symbols clashing cancel,
and fresh sound airing beckons.

Once again, a composer
attempts to match with notes
a beat that answers in conversation
on city street or on country road.

INOCULATING INTENSITY

A chuckle could be a foothold in history.
                              —Arundhati Roy

The path to sincerity choreographed
with punchlines waits for convergent noses.

Guffaws pull out stingers from the blows
that day and night introduce to cheeks.

A week after, the stepping stones,
each punctuated with a gulf on all sides,
tickle with irony and paradox.

A practiced comedic audience
in ballet slippers finesses little
on the feather-planted landing pads.

Lemmings in army boots march off edgy topics.

Every flight and fancy let down contends
with satellites dishes and infinite forks in the road.

Once butted, the cancan foreheads focus
with permission from Sarcasm Anonymous,

getting at, without a smirk,
brass tacks embedded in funny bones.

EVENT HORIZONS

Boredom with ready tears dreams of hangings.
—Charles Baudelaire

After fire hoses drench each spectacle
for details Dalmatians and ladders rest
against what remains behind.
Whole communities rollover
and light up cigarettes, while asking,
without alarm, "good for you?"

When time begins to crawl,
the calm between disasters
shifts from foot to foot.
The adrenaline gushes anticipate
within the first responder, regardless
that the ashes settle for news.

Whose 15-minutes for fame pay down the bills:
perpetrator, victim, or hero?
In capes, the trio bursts among the props
with lines and choreography memorized.

Meanwhile, nonchalance in rubber boots
and red suspenders strolls with senses
heightened for a story needing point of view
and for another day to whiz by.

ANGER MANAGEMENT

Every state storage chest
dispenses against anger.
Apathy apps and coping mechanisms
display for assurance
while the body performs robotics.

Shrugs, denial, amnesia spring
into action when the meme boys
in sandwich boards rough up intelligence
or the boss boots into order
to reboot for accounts.

The straight face slips on emoticons
and customer service scripts
and everyone laughs — right?

Distance, a running for the hills
burns from the hips and gut
the bitterness from around
bread and circus from around death
that then reroutes into good sports
and the standby, sex.

From a coast in Virginia,
Oregon frustrates enough
so that the drive anticipates to the end.
If a buffalo, learning to lean
on horns for the greater good
may reap after amber waves.

THE FLEE MARKET

Walking shoes and flotation devices
reply to the Trojan Horses riddled
in Benghazi, Aleppo, and Bagdad.
Seventy-seven raisins in a hand

assure on shore for a moment
that the strange and misunderstood emerge
behind, from the Mediterranean only.

Mid-day sidewalks will heave with nightmare,
and paradise will attempt walling against invasion.
To adjust actions, customs calibrate
upon the new backbone, within new flesh.

Berlin and Brussels bristle, quicks found
until from flight and fright wine
presses into water.

THE LONG TREK TO FREEDOM

Habits and customs stolen at gunpoint
or cratered into an early grave,
an address stripped from each body,
drape over a once paradisal landscape.

The walking dystopia in local shoes
and mirror image wishes for home,
while winter chills creep up spines
that watch along the asylum rout.

When fear suffocates before pity wakes,
before time caffeinates with understanding,
enmity spaces with jitters, slippery footing,
and prickly flesh if not with a beating from bats.

From biology, human nature jiu-jitsus
to listen, to learn, and to teach
among the babbling towers in cities
or lies on a jungle floor to spring from the brush.

INNOCENCE CERTIFICATE

Tickling expectations and inciting envy
until ephemeral pleasure drives for owners,
the ad-masters rally around the spiritual striptease
to commercial morals for the goods gods.

In neighborhoods, when not giggling and clapping,
the victims yawn for the assault: me, oh my!
Dionysus intrudes into the consumer orgy.

Sacrificial cities in a lottery mix
until drawn for the checker board map
New Orleans, New York, Flint.

Behind the buns and guns on screens,
the short-term culture between "no-longer"
and "not yet" bets with lives as chips chirp:
interregnum, interregnum.

FROM BONE SHOP MARINA

I gave that fat-head [Federico García Lorca] a shot in the head.
> —Antonio Benavides (as reported by Giles Tremlett)

The artist is approached not as an original thinker in his own medium but, rather, as an instinctive, intuitive executant, who, largely unaware of what he is doing, breaks through the mystery by the magic of his performance to 'express' truths the professionals think they can read better than he can himself.
> —Barnett Newman

The unfriendliness of society to his activity is difficult for the artist to accept.
> —Mark Rothko

1

Clouds formed into fog that gushed with blood
from 1900 through 1950 and ebbed
into small wars thereafter.

The first lightning flash struck in Dallas:
contingency slumped in a back seat.
Dishonest decades assumed
within the furniture in homes.

Easels and pencils had gathered for craft
while business models poked fun
and brushed against lips that question.

2

In mud, boots fill and did.
Beneath the heel, a nation,
gurgling in the monotonous sublime,

would not nose up to the impossible.

3

A crew waited for cliché, platitude,
and non-sequitur to reign enough
that the squawking and creaking
hulk lifted into a floating island.

4

While a known world ended
with each current event
on the 20th Century Limited,
drafts billowed and bellowed
as pages drifted with the colors.

5

The treasure in feet, in strokes
marks on the experience map:
within portside and starboard
and bow and stern mid-sea
freedom from tormenting
security and community.

6

Fathomed coastal and landlocked countries
harbor for schadenfreude, if not
for resentful gunship troops,
while mirroring the required secret smile.

Yet under the buzzwords, jingles,
and group think, each grin enforcer
flourishes while blind to the cost
and to the ticking in the clock.

7

The dog paddler Plato bobs
and mocks with cat calls
among the brainwashed
and now bloated bodies.

Should art die upon a swelling rage,
slaves were thrust upon the stage.

8

The raving market and propaganda
champagne christens until Koolaid disappears
and children sink into strait-jackets:

coloring book cemeteries
bubble with a vision for filling in.

9

Forever out of joint upon the SS Tomorrow,
a root network where gingerly blossoms,
human natures sit alone at breakfast tables
with attention toward traumatic imbalance
and bake, bathed in salt, soiled hands into evening.

10

Inventing balance for fear and anxiety,
desire and despair, chaos and horror,
Thumb Island, counterweight to technocracy
re-minds with huckleberry tendrils how to be.

11

When the canvases fill with breath
and the ambiguity in the shipping log
absorbs, the dove stretches

for the sailors so a bay outline, the X
on the cognitive map that hubris stole
only to hang around necks
promises now in human scale.

12

Famous for robots and cement shoes,
the underworld Laputa marches on
spouting dead images, hypnotic language.

On board an unmoored peninsula
for "land ho," all hands
from crow nest to the hold for the haul
sing for trireme schemes and for Queen Mary too.

SECTION NOTES

1. W. B. Yeats' "The Circus Animals Desertion" and his
    "toy Noah's ark" for the state of art now in twenty-first
    century. Robert Lowell's "Waking Early Sunday
    Morning" from *Near the Ocean* addresses the situation
    in the US as it did in Kennedy's and Johnson's time;
    W.H. Auden's "September 1, 1939."

2. Robert Lowell's "Waking Early Sunday Morning;"
    W.H. Auden's "September 1, 1939;" *1984* by George
    Orwell.

3. Jonathan Swift's *Gulliver's Travels*.

4. Hitchcock's phallic connotation with the train in *North
    by Northwest*.

5. Rothko's embrace of a kind of negative capability in his
    book *The Artist's Reality: Philosophies of Art*.

6. NA

7. Plato's banishment of poets as liars from *The Republic*
    with Boris Pasternak's understanding in poem "The
    Poet."

8. NA

9. Rescue ship in "Children of Men" by Alfonso Cuaron;
    "traumatic imbalance" Zizek's definition of life;
    reference to rhizome, Gille Deleuze.

10. *Snowpiercer* directed by Joon-ho Bong; Deleuze's rhizome via Twain's raft and Heidegger's shepherding being.

11. Noah's Ark; Samuel Tayor Coleridge's "The Rhyme of the Ancient Mariner."

12. Reference to Arthur Rimbaud's "Drunken Boat;" Jonathan Swift's *Gulliver's Travels*.

ASYLUM SEEKER

We have good people with good values who want to do the right
thing, but the structures of power that exist are working to their
own ends to extend their capability at the expense of the
freedoms of all.

—Edward Snowden

Such as we were we gave ourselves outright.

—Robert Frost

Poetry isn't revolution but a way of knowing why it must come.

—Adrienne Rich

I [have] no nation now but the imagination.

—Derek Walcott

1

The refugee squats at home —
three nations outside birthright.
Waiting for official exile status
fifty years after Dallas,
the mourning begins in earnest.

A spoon scrapes against the tin
for the last morsel.

2

During what bred and now circus,
the hedonists find that the cages open.
In turn for ignor-ance, paranoia
arms, taunts, and instigates.

Games for self-indulgence pierce
until a city for sacrifice comes around.

3

The indifferent surroundings,
also distracted by totem and taboo,
pummel with nickel and dime
the reliable target that patches
together a work week tattooed
to the nervous system —
Saturday bets to catch up
to animals in the streets ambush.

4

Without experiencing abandonment
that makes words, the just do it arts
enact as an engine sweeping aside
brambles holding a bud:
sheep traumatized in the mall maw,
one-upping, unable to honor life.

The wolf in a shepherd's skin peddles.

5

At sunset since 13, the foreigner crawls
between the flapless map:
"This Administration intends
to be candid about its errors…,"
and, penned within a pen,
reads for sleep while stars weep.

ACKNOWLEDGMENTS

antiBODY Anthology: "Dead See Scroll"
Assonance Literary Magazine: "Lying Around"
Backlash Review: "Inoculating Intensity"
BlazeVox: "The Nobility of Our Existence" and "This Sad Time
We Must Obey"
Carcinogenetic Poetry: "Yours = Mine" and "Snap Shot for
Zoe"
Clockwise Cat: "Bustle Hustle"
Eunoia Review: "Google Drive."
Former People: "Todestrieb and the Parasite," "Sand Trap," and
"Domestication"
Futures Trading: "The Flee Market"
Harbinger Asylum: "Brainwash," "Event Horizon," "Frontal
Lobe to Psychology," and "Latest Trend"
Ibbetson Street Press: "Feed Force"
Otoliths: "Chestnut Frame"
Pennsylvania Review: "Wearing Identification," "Fatal Flaws,"
"Lactation Nation," and "Global Societies"
Poydras Review: "An Alzheimer Bank Rolled In" and "In the
Morass"
Review Americana: "From Bone Shop Marina"
Rumble: "Work Quirk"
Sein und Werden: "Surveillance for Any Era"
Stark: "Asylum Seeker"
Synesthesia Literary Journal: "Distant Destiny"
Syzygy: "Second Nature"
Two Thirds North: "The Tub Suds Soap Opera"

Many thanks to Leslie Kreiner Wilson

ABOUT THE AUTHOR

Rich Murphy's credits include four other books: *The Apple in the Monkey Tree* (Codhill Press), *Voyeur* 2008 Gival Press Poetry Award (Gival Press), *Americana* 2013 Prize Americana (The Poetry Press of Press Americana), and *Body Politic* (Prolific Press). He has published five chapbooks: *Great Grandfather* (Pudding House Press), *Family Secret* (Finishing Line Press), *Hunting and Pecking* (Ahadada Books), *Phoems for Mobile Vices* (BlazeVox), and *Paideia* (Aldrich Press).

Recent prose scholarship on poetics has been published in *The International Journal of the Humanities, Reconfigurations: A Journal of Poetry and Poetics, The Journal of Ecocriticism, The New Directions in the Humanities Journal*, and *New Writing: The International Journal for the Practice and Theory of Creative Writing*. Rich has taught academic and creative writing at several colleges and universities.